Praise for Nicole Mc

"Tolstoy famously began his great novel 'Happy families are all alike; every unhappy family is unhappy in its own way.' Nicole McCarthy's electrifying book—a hybrid of poem, essay, photo, document, lyric and elegy—shows that every modern divorce is painful in its own way. Anna Karenina struggles against the social constraints of pre-feminist culture of 19th century Russia, but the woman in *A Summoning* faces the more insidious enemy of American cultural schizophrenia: sexual repression vs sex positive sloganeering; hedonism vs puritanism; militarism vs slacker culture. The clash of the desire for home and the desire for freedom, whatever those mean … McCarthy's book is fearless, brave and a godsend to readers.

—Rebecca Brown, author of *The Gifts of the Body* (winner of a LAMBDA Literary award) and *Not Heaven, Somewhere Else*

"Nicole McCarthy's *A Summoning* is an elegant, unflinching treatise on the subject of memory, engaging everything from the celestially studded mythos of ancient Greece to newfound conclusions of cellular biology to coax forth the intricacies of reminiscence. The searing prose and arresting visuals of the hybrid form are nothing short of orchestral in McCarthy's hands. Blueprints reveal the architecture of toxic domesticity. Textual repetition and erasure lay bare the devastating unreliability with which we bear witness and lay claim to one another. *A Summoning* truly soars, however, when McCarthy grants the reader vulnerable access to an airless and seemingly inescapable love affair. When trauma infiltrates the house of memory, *A Summoning* suggests, sometimes the only thing to do is burn it down. As she escapes these smoking rooms, McCarthy offers by example this amazing grace: that holy reclamation of the self is possible. That if in our darkest hours we find a way to persist, we will remain."

—Piper J. Daniels, author of *Ladies Lazarus*, finalist for a LAMBDA Literary award and a PEN/Diamonstein-Spielvogel Award

"In her gorgeous debut, Nicole McCarthy takes us through the rooms of a life, warning that there are rooms we won't wish to revisit, places that we will flee, destroy, set aflame. Memory, she instructs, is not so much a palace as it is a haunted attic, a storage shed of despair, places we return to against our wishes, a drink we are forced to take. 'Would you alter a memory, if you could?' she asks. In a fragile and ethereal layering of poetic language, intense recollections, philosophical propositions, and visual splicing and collaging, McCarthy alters our understanding of the method of loci and thereby the notion that memory is a palace. She has set it down here, permanently, and for all time, in this book, so as to remind us that no matter how crumbling, how collapsed our lives, we can only hope to escape our frantic pacing, our retracings through memory."

—Jenny Boully, author of *Betwixt-and-Between*, *The Body*, and others

"The way architects understand that structures act on us as much as we act on them, Nicole McCarthy has written and designed a living book that functions like a building containing separate but overlapping rooms of body, memory, and space. Each room, no matter how complex, is accessible from anywhere in this building, and that's why *A Summoning* is alive and gracious, because I feel like it cares about how we move through and inhabit its spaces. We can participate like hell in this book and it's a beautiful thing to have that type of intellectual and emotional agency."

—Steven Dunn, author of *water & power* and *Potted Meat*

"Asking, 'can I give up this body when I have filled it with too many memories?' McCarthy shows us where they truly reside—under shoulder blade and rib, in the taut muscles of calves still ready to sprint away from what taunts and haunts them. Kneading the places where love, loss, and trauma reside, she risks recall to help us reckon with the power Mnemosyne holds over us."

—Amaranth Borsuk, author of *The Book* and *Pomegranate Eater*

"Nicole McCarthy extends and perforates the essay form with this insistence: to reclaim what has been taken, to build back memories that have been gaslit, to re-introduce the body into architectures of living, you need all manners of writing and thought. You need blueprints and fragmentation; you need the white of the page, the line breaking, the flow of prose, the simultaneous silence and noise of erasure. The resulting shape is a series of built spaces made for healing and self-articulation. *A Summoning* is a vital work and an admirable debut."

—Renee Gladman, author of *Calamities* and the Ravicka Series

A
SUMMONING

HEAVY FEATHER REVIEW

Cover Design: Katie Prince
Interior Art: Nicole McCarthy

Book Design by Jason Teal

Heavy Feather Review
Manhattan, KS 66502
heavyfeatherreview.org

1st Printing: 2022

ISBN-13 978-1-955390-03-3

For G + G McCarthy

Think of two people, living together day after day,
year after year, in this small space…bumping against each
other's bodies by mistake or on purpose, sensually,
aggressively, awkwardly, impatiently, in rage or in love—
think what deep though invisible tracks they must leave,
everywhere, behind them—
Christopher Isherwood
A Single Man

2013: My husband, R, is home.

He squeezes in next to me in the booth, real close. I can smell his cologne again. We'd run away to the ocean to a small inn we love, one we return to after every deployment. We need to bridge the intimacy we shared before he left, with the strange familiarity we now experience—when you know someone so well but haven't touched or interacted in an extended period of time. My cheeks flush when our arms graze each other— eyes meet, locking in a longing we've been trying to define for years.

I swish through photos on my phone, showing him what he missed. I don't need to show him [he knows already] but every time he insists, I think, because the pain of not being here helps him be present when he is home.

One summer I had hair that stretched down toward my navel and I was desperate to cut it off. I sent him pictures of short bobs that I'd been obsessing over, dreaming of summers without drizzled hair wrapping around my neck.

"Please don't cut your hair, not at least until I come home."

Why should I have to wait? What difference could it make? He left with the memory of me with long brown hair he'd comb fingers through in the winter before resting it on my neck, insulated from the cold. He knew change was inevitable, things were going to carry on here with or without him and little was within his control. He clung to the memory of the wife he left behind, silently crying in the airport with hair cascading down as a shield. Returning home to a short black-bobbed woman would have felt jarring and foreign; a symbol that the clock hadn't stopped. Consistency was necessary to his memory to stay safe and regulated while overseas. Two weeks after he returned, I cut it all off.

We spend the weekend walking the boardwalks of the beach, his fingertips grazing my naked neck.

The word 'memory' stems from the Greek word 'Mnemosyne,' which bore the Greek titan goddess of the same name. Daughter of Uranus and Gaea, and mother to the nine muses (Zeus being the father), Mnemosyne is one of the most prominent and powerful characters in early Greek theology.

Often, characters in early Greek literature became possessed by Mnemosyne, creating a conduit of sorts, to reflect on personal and cultural events that she had documented from the past.

Her existence was actively present in both their daily lives and their after-lives. When individuals died and encountered the God of the Underworld, Hades, their souls approached two rivers: Lethe and Mnemosyne. Before being reincarnated, they would be given the choice to drink from either river: Lethe effectively clearing the slate and erasing your past lives; or Mnemosyne, giving the individual omniscient qualities to remember elements of former lives.

Human memories form and exist on a cellular level. Associations link one neuron to another and another, making a pattern of neurons linking and firing in the auditory cortex of the brain. These patterns of neurons fire when an initial stimulus triggers a memory. As we sleep, our hippocampus relays information and moments back and forth to the cortex, etching the details into a more permanent status. This process, called consolidation, is how short-term memories are converted and preserved as long-term memories.

Our memories are divided up into four distinct categories, depending on their context.

Procedural memory, stored in the cerebellum and putamen, contains details on everyday actions, such as riding a bike, brushing your teeth, or writing with a pen in your hand.

Semantic memories race back and forth from your cortex to your frontal lobes as you try to recall your mother's maiden name, the state capitol of Florida, or the hours of your favorite cafe. Semantic memory is rooted in fact, laid down by your cortex as useful information to preserve (in theory).

Episodic memories bring forth experiences in our lives we're recollecting, prompted or unprompted. When our senses are activated, be it by smell or sound, neurons in our cortex begin firing with the hippocampus before bringing some form of the memory forward.

The last category of memory resides in the amygdala. Instantaneous and striking, these memories bypass the standard process of consolidation through the hippocampus, foregoing long-term storage in the cortex. The amygdala is the house of trauma and fear.

*

There is a personal and universal context to all our memories.

Collectively we remember national events, accomplishments, and tragedies together. We remember who we were with, where we were when these moments occurred, etc. We recollect speeches of our forefathers and speeches of our actual fathers. We play trivia games with each other about how long the Mississippi River is, or how long it's been since you've seen your aging grandparents. Our brains file these memories away, personal and universal, depending on the circumstance of the event.

coulda
woulda
shoulda

co
b
t

Regional Hospital

he
would
have
come
for
you

"It's ok, you don't have to come

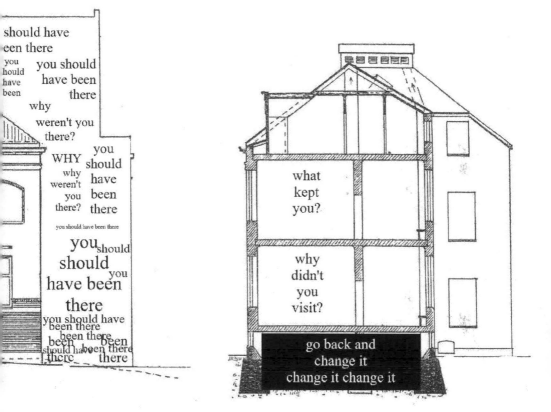

should have
een there

you   you should
hould   have been
have
been   there

        why

    weren't you
      there?

            you
    WHY should
    why   have
   weren't been
    you
   there? there

        you should have been there

        you should
    should   you
    have been
        there

      you should have
        been there
        been there
    been   been
   should have been there
      there   there

what
kept
you?

why
didn't
you
visit?

go back and
change it
change it change it

When I was growing up my dad was perpetually boisterous—his voice boomed from his chest, a thunder all his own that I knew all my life. In anger or disbelief or elation, it always felt barely contained in his body, like his skin held back the form it needed to take to possess a room.

Unsteady with love, but rich in its masculinity, his voice was a constant in my tiny world of change.

In my early 20s, we chased a diagnosis that left my dad uncomfortably overweight, lacking sleep, and without a voice for over a year. At restaurants, the waiters had to lean in to hear his order over quiet dinner chatter. He never wanted us to order for him. His laughter existed only in a rasp and a silent, stretching smile. He couldn't talk to us on the phone anymore. I had resigned my body to think I would never hear his voice again.

Towards the end, the will to care seemed to vacate his body; he stood outside on his porch, smoke escaping his lips, as he whispered to his children:

"Nice of your aunts to visit. Randomly," he says. I nod.

"Will you put the trash out on the—" louder, straining, "put the TRASH OUT ON THE CURB FOR ME?" I nod.

"Want to go out to dinner with them while they're here?"

"I don't know. Not really up for it anymore." A shrug existed as surrender.

" ———————— "

Seeing his warm breath hit the cold night air was the only indication to me that he was still alive.

My aunts flew up from California to spend time with him and, perhaps, to say goodbye.

He was out of doctors. He was out of work. He was out of money.

Existing in a pre-literacy era, the Greeks only understood the retention of knowledge through memorization. When learning a new skill, familial story, or cultural anecdote, the townsmen channeled Mnemosyne to assist the recollection process. Men were trained to 'exercise' their brains daily in an effort to strengthen their memory; to carry the mental burden of remembering.

The complete history of their society existed solely in the minds of men.

Sitting around a bonfire, men would regale families and friends with adventurous tales set to music and meter. Men would follow the musicality of each epic, built into a hexameter rhythm, filling in blanks as they went. Through constant repetition and rhyming, literary and cultural traditions were preserved through performative recitation.

Memories that haven't gone through the consolidation process yet are like clay waiting to dry—they're vulnerable to malleability.

The process most damaging to memories is recall. Every time we call upon a memory for our own personal use or to share with others, what we remember, however, is not THE picture of the event but A picture. The same neurons fire and bring forth every element that composes the moment, but the details are indistinct.

When you relive a memory, perhaps you give the impression of more confidence than you originally had, you act like someone didn't bother you, when in reality they did. When the memory goes back into storage your hippocampus re-writes the memory to add your edits before storing it in the cortex. If it's ever recalled again, your brain may only showcase the new and improved memory you tampered with before.

The only record of Mnemosyne, her muses, and their gifts appear in Hesiod's Theogony (7th Century B.C.), an epic poem in which the narrator documents the history and spectacle surrounding the titans and gods who reside over Greece. The significance in this case is *Theogony* is one of very few texts documenting Greek theology of gods and titans, including Homer's *Odyssey*. Mnemosyne played a crucial role in documenting memory in the oral tradition, and here Hesiod transferred that knowledge in written form in order to preserve her legacy of memory keeping.

But as their civilization developed, and letters were introduced as a new form of knowledge retention, Mnemosyne's function in their lives inevitably faded.

Has a moment ever haunted you?

Maybe you recollect a moment often to muddle the details or you hope it dissipates over time. Would you alter a memory, if you could?

I relive a moment of hesitation all the time. A moment of guarded contemplation. A regret of immobility. Maybe, after years of believing I had done it differently, it'll be so.

MANIPULATE.
[2009: boyfriend, "H"]

I pick you up from your friend's wedding in the backwoods of Buckley. You wouldn't come out of the venue hall; lips locked with your favorite glass of whiskey.

My head is pounding from the night before; my 21st run on the town, the one you weren't invited to. I pull up to our farmhouse and the distance you keep from my body, normally the plea I wake with on my lips, vanishes as your anger becomes known. I feel it tremoring up my spine; my hands start to shake.

You corner me in the house, outside eyes no longer watching, holding you accountable. You tell me I embarrassed you at the wedding, hung over and looking wrecked, leaving early for temporary convalescence. I'm not behaving how a woman should. You force me to my knees to beg for forgiveness, for understanding. To beg for you to keep me.

You begin to unbutton your tux. My muscles tense and I start to sweat, a chain reaction set in motion whenever you undress in front of me now. I look at the tux, how it sits awkwardly on your overweight frame, tight and unnatural.

You force me to beg for a wedding ring, one I know I don't want anymore, a fact I haven't worked up the heart [or spine] to tell you. You yell that the figures we witnessed standing in that church today making vows could have been us, if only I'd been the exact type of woman you want. I've been crying but you just notice. You cup my face, your calloused fingers running the line of my jaw, a moment of tenderness you give as if I'm thirsting for it, before asking me to take my clothes off.

We have to fix this, you say.

I sob as the breath I held escapes from my chest. You lower me down onto you in the middle of our living room, your tux pants pulled down to your ankles. You don't allow me to be passive;

I can't lie here waiting for your release, legs lackadaisically around your body. You force me to ride you and never ask me to stop crying.

It's July—the setting sun pours in through the south windows. I can hear the horses on the farm running through tall grass. The apple trees just outside the living room window are bearing fruit and gnats have begun to convene around the drooping branches. I feel you run your fingers possessively over my hips and up my glistening back.

When you finish, you help me off of you and then grab water from the fridge. You clean your guns while watching a movie I hate. Your posture the status of indifference.

I throw up my lunch and skip dinner, avoiding whatever room you enter.

Researchers early on introduced the Interference Theory, proving how simple it is to plant a memory in someone else's memory bank. Through a series of experiments, scientists showed videos to patients followed by a list of questions. By opening the discussions with misleading questions and reports, they confused the subjects into thinking events occurred in the video that never actually happened. The test subjects were convinced they were right until they were shown the videos again.

Gaslighting is another term for memory tampering. Often appearing in abusive relationships, or exploited by sociopaths and narcissists, gaslighting is the blatant manipulation of someone else's memory. The events of firm long-term memories are denied by one person, resulting in the victim questioning the credibility of their own memory. This protects the guilty party and prevents the innocent from coming forward with evidence or accusations.

Our hippocampus is always at work storing memories for short- and long-term use. There is nothing to protect us from false or misleading memories being planted by others or by ourselves.

*

October 2016: my husband, R, received orders to relocate to New Jersey. I put my thesis on memory away while I wrapped up a house overflowing with it.

Our whole relationship exists in this house—I can feel it breathing in every room I walk through.

Our memory palace is disintegrating before our eyes and by our hands. In selling, we are evicting memories, leaving them to fade and be overridden by others.

These spaces that house our lives become territories of activation. Milestones of the mundane and extraordinary occur within certain walls, memories that cannot be replicated or packed with care to move to another location.

Moving the dresser to stage the house I find dried rose petals from when he proposed. We wipe down tree sap off of vaulted ceilings from Christmas after Christmas of fifteen-foot trees. Carpet fibers trap and trace a life.

I lament for weeks, torn by the thrill of a life on the East Coast and the desire to maintain comfort on the West Coast.

"All our memories are contained in this house," I tell him, "It's hard to let it go."

"We'll make new memories then. That's not something we'll ever stop doing."

*

R has been in the military for over a decade now. Throughout our relationship, he's been sent overseas almost every year for months at a time. In the beginning it devastated me—I'd crumble in on myself at every missed video chat or extended return date.

Then he deployed again.

Then he deployed again.

And it got easier.

He missed birthdays. He missed anniversaries. He missed parties. He missed my readings. He missed holidays. He missed every days.

He missed ~~28 months~~. 34 months.

I've made many memories while he was away, and after a while he could feel the void he left, could almost see the space in the frame left open for him. And then after more time he realized I was no longer leaving space for his body.

Every time he came home, it was as if the memories he accumulated while away were off the table. He'd be desperate to go on a weekend trip to the ocean, or plan a date night in the city—anything to begin the process of making up for all the moments he missed.

He takes me on vacations while he's home, transporting our state of mind from deployment life to post-deployment-lets-try-hard-for-normalcy life. 'Let's take a picture' rolls off his tongue with every other breath. Each trip he hopes will produce pictures that will replace every frame/every profile image/every evidence of the life I've led without him here.

We can live and linger forever inside a frame.

"When was this photo taken?"

"Who were you with here?"

"I wonder what country I was in then."

Am I a memory romantic?

I'm a ghost unwilling to leave these shared spaces after everyone else has vacated. My husband left toward his new residence without a second glance back at the house we shared for six years. I sit in front of the fireplace, in our hollow home, crying over all that's bound to be lost.

*

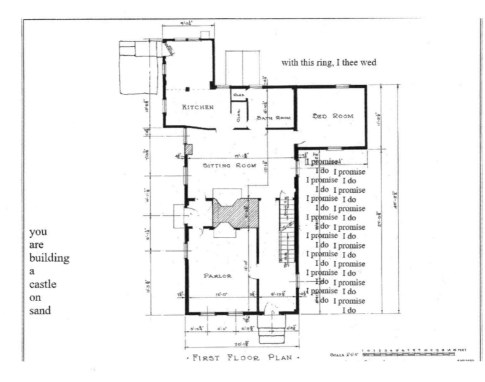

with this ring, I thee wed

KITCHEN

BATH ROOM

BED ROOM

SITTING ROOM

PARLOR

you
are
building
a
castle
on
sand

I promise
I do I promise
I promise I do
I do I promise
I promise I do
I do I promise
I promise I do
I do I promise
I promise I do
I do I promise
I promise I do
I do I promise
I promise I do
I do I promise
I promise I do
I do I promise
I do

· FIRST FLOOR PLAN ·

SCALE

As the memory of Mnemosyne faded gradually, and cognitive exercises were traded for linguistic studies, one individual was quite vocal about his distrust of a written language. In *The Phaedrus*, Plato argues the debilitating effects written discourse will have on their community and on the world: "it will introduce forgetfulness into the soul of those who learn it: they will not practice using their memory because they will put their trust in writing…you have not discovered the potion for remembering, but for reminding."

He considered the movement toward memory documentation a weakness, a move that would deteriorate the ability to recollect facts and events going forward.

Plato was romanced by the fluidity of memory—the recollection or recitation of memory presented a movement in the mind, allowing room for revision and improvisation when necessary. Documenting these occasions in writing, he speculated, cemented the moments forever, removing the opportunity for revision or influence. These "fixed, formalized" records hindered an individual's creativity in the process.

*

Sometimes memories overlap. Bleed into each other like merging rivulets.

Why is it my joyful memories are hazy and muddled together, overlapping and envious of space, but the painful ones are so singular, so distinct. I can feel their rough edges, on a page break all to themselves. They take up more room in my body, space I cannot seem to control. They hide behind intestines, just out of reach, or in stretch marks lingering on my thighs. Even my uterus offers a place of refuge.

Can I give up this body when I have filled it with too many memories?

Can I clear the slate then?

et at the coffee shop i hate on st.
s ave in tacoma. we sat across
you. there was dirt under your
r nails and dark rings around
eyes. you asked me how finals
nodding and listening with
t. or care. or maybe apathy.

u slid miniature bottles of tequila & rum across the table, then said you couldn't be
ends with us anymore. i had your christmas present in my purse. i was livid, and yelled,
ink. you just sat there and took it. our espressos arrived and we paused:

> then you said
> again, she
> won't let you
> be friends with
> us. when you
> hugged us
> goodbye, why
> did you smile?
> what did i
> miss?

it was raining. no. it was sunny this time. It was july. you held my hand on your favorite couch. steam was r

from the coffee cup in your other hand. your eyes wiggled now when you focused on an object/subject. you s

comes with age. i asked to hear your stories from the war again, knowing it would be the last. you smiled.

pointed to a picture of me on your favorite coffee table and said i was your angel. the hearing aids you empl

whistled from your ears often. you told me the stories this time. i think, then attempted to rise to make break

our round belly was gone; you were swimming in your sweaters. your knees shook, even with braces. you ha

dinner that night with us, then died in september.

we met at the coffee shop i hate on st.
helens ave in tacoma. we sat across
from you. there was dirt under your
finger nails and dark rings around
your eyes. you asked me how finals
went, nodding and listening with
intent. or care. or maybe apathy.

you slid miniature bottles of tequila & rum across the table, then said you couldn't be
friends with us anymore. i had your christmas present in my purse. i was livid, and yelled,
i think. you just sat there and took it. our espressos arrived and we paused:
then you said
again, she
won't let you
be friends with
us. when you
hugged us
goodbye, why
did you smile?
what did i
miss?

when i learned i could
be a human being alone

s raining. no. it was sunny this time. It was july. you held my hand on your favorite couch. steam was rising

i sat in a museum
in seattle

he coffee cup in your other hand. your eyes wiggled now when you focused on an object/subject. you said it

the rain beat down
on the windows lights flickered

es with age. i asked to hear your stories from the war again, knowing it would be the last. you smiled. you

from the storm and i encountered
martha rosler and

ed to a picture of me on your favorite coffee table and said i was your angel. the hearing aids you employed

kehinde wiley and
_____ and

led from your ears often. you told me the stories this time, i think, then attempted to rise to make breakfast.

i was getting your texts
but i kept pushing them

ind belly was gone; you were swimming in your sweaters. your knees shook, even with braces. you had a full

back into my purse
dinner that night with us, then died in september.

et at the coffee shop i hate on st.
s ave in tacoma. we sat across
you. there was dirt under your
r nails and dark rings around
eyes. you asked me how finals
nodding and listening with
t. or care. or maybe apathy.

u slid miniature bottles of tequila & rum across the table, then said you couldn't be
nds with us anymore. i had your christmas present in my purse. i was livid, and yelled,
then you said
ink. you just sat there and took it. our espressos arrived and we paused:
again, she
won't let you
be friends with
us. when you
hugged us
goodbye, why
did you smile?
what did i
miss?

it was raining. no. it was sunny this time. it was july. you held my hand on your favorite couch. steam was r

when i learned i could
be a human being alone

from the coffee cup in your other hand. your eyes wiggled now when you focused on an object/subject. you s

i sat in a museum
in seattle

comes with age. i asked to hear your stories from the war again, knowing it would be the last. you smiled.

the rain beat down
on the windows lights flickered

pointed to a picture of me on your favorite coffee table and said i was your angel. the hearing aids you empl

from the storm and i encountered
martha rosler and
kehinde wiley and
_____ and

whistled from your ears often. you told me the stories this time, i think, then attempted to rise to make break

i was getting your texts
but i kept pushing them

our round belly was gone; you were swimming in your sweaters. your knees shook, even with braces. you ha

back into my purse
dinner that night with us, then died in september.

it was noon on a wednesday. those days we lived
in a salt-rimmed existence. the margaritas
ping-ponged around our shaking bodies,
giggling. in darkness, we laid on the floor in our
tiny campus office. we wrote a poem to explain/
to capture/ to tell someone (maybe us) why
these events were happening/ were justifiable at
that moment. that was in may.
i saw you last week. finally. we hadn't yet
forgotten about it.

we met at the coffee shop i hate on st.
helens ave in tacoma. we sat across
from you. there was dirt under your
finger nails and dark rings around
your eyes. you asked me how finals
tequila. it's always tequila. a trifecta of tequila.
went, nodding and listening with
polaroids from movie theater photo booths dry
intent. or care. or maybe apathy.
in our pockets as our livers sip slowly from
happy hour sangrias.

you slid miniature bottles of tequila & rum across the table, then said you couldn't be
friends with us anymore. i had your christmas present in my purse. i was livid, and yelled,
then you said
i think. you just sat there and took it. our espressos arrived and we paused:
again, she

won't let you
be friends with
us. when you
hugged us
goodbye, why
did you smile?
what did i
miss?

when i learned i could
be a human being alone

s raining. no. it was sunny this time. It was july. you held my hand on your favorite couch. steam was rising

i sat in a museum
in seattle

he coffee cup in your other hand. your eyes wiggled now when you focused on an object/subject. you said it

the rain beat down
on the windows lights flickered

es with age. i asked to hear your stories from the war again, knowing it would be the last. you smiled. you

ed to a picture of me on your favorite coffee table and said i was your angel. the hearing aids you employed

martha rosler and   are you

kehinde wiley and   my

led from your ears often. you told me the stories this time, i think, then attempted to rise to make breakfast.   understudy father?

_____ and

i was getting your texts   will you

und belly was gone; you were swimming in your sweaters. your knees shook, even with braces. you had a full   fill the role

but i kept pushing them

back into my purse   when he inevitably

dinner that night with us, then died in september.   calls in sick?

i shake the hands
of your colleagues
you introduce me
with memorized stats

it was noon on a wednesday. those days we lived
in a salt-rimmed existence. the margaritas
ping-ponged around our shaking bodies,
giggling. in darkness, we laid on the floor in our
tiny campus office. we wrote a poem to explain/
to capture/ to tell someone (maybe us) why
these events were happening/ were justifiable at
that moment. that was in may.
i saw you last week. finally. we hadn't yet
forgotten about it.

et at the coffee shop i hate on st.
s ave in tacoma. we sat across
you. there was dirt under your
r nails and dark rings around
eyes. you asked me how finals
, nodding and listening with
. or care. or maybe apathy.
ur pockets as our livers sip slowly from

it's always tequila. a trifecta of tequila.
ids from movie theater photo booths dry
happy hour sangrias

i slid miniature bottles of tequila & rum across the table, then said you couldn't be
ends with us anymore. i had your christmas present in my purse. i was livid, and yelled,
ink, you just sat there and took it. our espressos arrived and we paused:
then you said
again, she

won't let you
be friends with
us. when you
hugged us
goodbye, why
did you smile?
what did i
miss?

when i learned i could
be a human being alone

i sat in a museum
in seattle

the rain beat down
on the windows lights flickered
from the storm and i encountered
martha rosler and
kehinde wiley and
_____ and
i was getting your texts
but i kept pushing them
back into my purse

it was raining. no. it was sunny this time. It was july. you held my hand on your favorite couch. steam was r
from the coffee cup in your other hand. your eyes wiggled now when you focused on an object/subject. you s
comes with age. i asked to hear your stories from the war again, knowing it would be the last. you smiled.
pointed to a picture of me on your favorite coffee table and said i was your angel. the hearing aids you empl
whistled from your ears often. you told me the stories this time, i think, then attempted to rise to make break
our round belly was gone; you were swimming in your sweaters. your knees shook, even with braces. you ha
dinner that night with us, then died in september.

are you
my
understudy father?

will you
fill the role
when he inevitably
calls in sick?

i shake the hands
of your colleagues
you introduce me
with memorized stats

it was noon on a wednesday. those days we lived
in a salt-rimmed existence. the margaritas
ping-ponged around our shaking bodies,
giggling. in darkness, we laid on the floor in our
tiny campus office. we wrote a poem to explain/
to capture/ to tell someone (maybe us) why
these events were happening/ were justifiable at
that moment. that was in may.
i saw you last week. finally. we hadn't yet
forgotten about it.

we met at the coffee shop i hate on st.
helens ave in tacoma. we sat across
from you. there was dirt under your
finger nails and dark rings around
your eyes. you asked me how finals
went, nodding and listening with
intent. or care. or maybe apathy.

tequila. it's always tequila. a trifecta of tequila.
polaroids from movie theater photo booths dry
in our pockets as our livers sip slowly from
happy hour sangrias

you slid miniature bottles of tequila & rum across the table, then said you couldn't be
friends with us anymore. i had your christmas present in my purse. i was livid, and yelled,
i think. you just sat there and took it. our espressos arrived and we paused.
then you said
again, she
won't let you
be friends with
us. when you
hugged us
goodbye, why
did you smile?
what did i
miss?

again.
ed a hand up my skirt. your mother was calling, then she called again.
uld feel my makeup run in the august heat. on the way home, you
u found me before picking up your bags. You said i was beautiful. i
lled from the plane to say you landed at mcchord. i heard your voices in
the automatic doors flew open. i hadn't worn underwear that day. you
wn in the passenger terminal at mcchord. my skirt fluttered up every
eat collected at the crooks of my knees. i paced/sat down/paced/sat

when i learned i could
s raining. no. it was sunny this time. it was july. you held my hand on your favorite couch. steam was rising
be a human being alone

i sat in a museum
the coffee cup in your other hand. your eyes wiggled now when you focused on an object/subject. you said it
in seattle

the rain beat down
nes with age. i asked to hear your stories from the war again, knowing it would be the last. you smiled. you
on the windows lights flickered

from the storm and i encountered
ted to a picture of me on your favorite coffee table and said i was your angel. the hearing aids you employed
martha rosler and

kehinde wiley and
tled from your ears often. you told me the stories this time, i think, then attempted to rise to make breakfast.
_____ and

i was getting your texts
und belly was gone; you were swimming in your sweaters. your knees shook, even with braces. you had a ful
but i kept pushing them
back into my purse
dinner that night with us, then died in september. will you

are you
my
understudy father?
fill the role
when he inevitably
calls in sick?
i shake the hands
of your colleagues

I pay a stranger to touch me
and i'm reminded
again
how it feels
to be human
in possession
of a body.

it was noon on a wednesday. those days we lived
in a salt-rimmed existence. the margaritas
ping-ponged around our shaking bodies,
giggling. in darkness, we laid on the floor in our
tiny campus office. we wrote a poem to explain/
to capture/ to tell someone (maybe us) why
these events were happening/ were justifiable at
that moment. that was in may.
i saw you last week. finally. we hadn't yet
forgotten about it.

you introduce those
with memorized truths
about us
academic addicts
what is this feeling
like a heavy covering
keening
afraid

net at the coffee shop i hate on st.
ns ave in tacoma. we sat across
you. there was dirt under your
r nails and dark rings around
eyes. you asked me how finals

again.

la. it's always tequila. a trifecta of tequila.
, nodding and listening with
oids from movie theater photo booths dry.
t. or care. or maybe apathy.
ur pockets as our livers sip slowly from
happy hour sangrias.

u slid miniature bottles of tequila & rum across the table, then said you couldn't be
ends with us anymore. i had your christmas present in my purse. i was livid, and yelled,
then you said
think, you just sat there and took it. our espressos arrived and we paused.

won't let you
be friends with
us. when you
hugged us
goodbye, why
did you smile?
what did i
miss?

slipped a hand up my skirt. your mother was calling, then she called again.
could feel my makeup run in the august heat. on the way home, you
you found me before picking up your bags. you said i was beautiful. i
again, she
called from the plane to say you landed. i heard your voice. i—
time the automatic doors flew open. i hadn't worn underwear that day, you
down in the passenger terminal at mcchord. my skirt fluttered up every
sweat collected at the crooks of my knees. i paced/sat down/paced/sat

when i learned i could
be a human being alone

it was raining. no. it was sunny this time. it was july. you held my hand on your favorite couch. steam was

i sat in a museum
in seattle

from the coffee cup in your other hand. your eyes wiggled now when you focused on an object/subject. you

the rain beat down
on the windows lights flickered

comes with age. i asked to hear your stories from the war again, knowing it would be the last. you smiled.

from the storm and i encountered

pointed to a picture of me on your favorite coffee table and said i was your angel. the hearing aids you emp

martha rosler and
kehinde wiley and
_____ and

whistled from your ears often. you told me the stories this time. i think, then attempted to rise to make brea

i was getting your texts
but i kept pushing them
back into my purse

your round belly was gone; you were swimming in your sweaters. your knees shook, even with braces. you ha

dinner that night with us, then died in september.

are you
my
understudy father?
will you
fill the role
when he inevitably
calls in sick?
i shake the hands
of your colleagues

I pay a stranger to touch me
and i'm reminded
again
how it feels
to be human
in possession
of a body.

it was noon on a wednesday. those days we liv
in a salt-rimmed existence. the margaritas
ping-ponged around our shaking bodies,
giggling. in darkness, we laid on the floor in
tiny campus office. we wrote a poem to expla
to capture/ to tell someone (maybe us) why
these events were happening/ were justifiable
that moment. that was in may.
i saw you last week. finally. we hadn't yet
forgotten about it.

we met at the coffee shop i hate on st.
helens ave in tacoma. we sat across
from you. there was dirt under your
finger nails and dark rings around
your eyes. you asked me how finals
went, nodding and listening with
intent. or care. or maybe apathy.
you slid miniature bottles of tequila & rum across the table, then said you couldn't be
friends with us anymore. i had your christmas present in my purse. i was livid, and yelled,
again, she
i think, you just sat there and took it. our espressos arrived and we paused.

won't let you
be friends with
us. when you
hugged us
goodbye, why
did you smile?
what did i
miss?

out of the dark
& towards you
2500 miles
2500 miles
2500 miles
2500 miles
2500 miles
2500 miles
2500 miles
2500 miles
you sent a flashlight

when i learned i could
be a human being alone

s raining. no. it was sunny this time. It was july. you held my hand on your favorite couch. steam was rising

i sat in a museum
in seattle

he coffee cup in your other hand. your eyes wiggled now when you focused on an object/subject. you said it

the rain beat down
on the windows lights flickered

es with age. i asked to hear your stories from the war again, knowing it would be the last. you smiled. you

from the storm and i encountered

ed to a picture of me on your favorite coffee table and said i was your angel. the hearing aids you employed

martha rosler and

kehinde wiley and

led from your ears often. you told me the stories this time, i think, then attempted to rise to make breakfast.

_____ and

i was getting your texts

are you

nd belly was gone; you were swimming in your sweaters. your knees shook, even with braces. you had a full

but i kept pushing them

my

understudy father?

back into my purse

dinner that night with us, then died in september. will you

fill the role
when he inevitably
calls in sick?

I pay a stranger to touch me
and i'm reminded
again
how it feels
to be human
in possession
of a body.

i shake the hands
of your colleagues
you introduce me
with memorized stats
about shaking bodies,

it was noon on a wednesday those days we lived
in a salt-rimmed existence. the margaritas
ping-ponged around our
giggling. in darkness, we
tiny campus office. we wrote a poem to explain/
to capture/ to tell someone (maybe us) why
these events were happening
that moment. that was in may.
i saw you last week.
forgotten about it.

academia. laid on the floor in our
what is this telling me
office. waves come and going
in aiding/ were justifiable at
keeping me
afloat. finally. we hadn't yet

et at the coffee shop i hate on st.
s ave in tacoma. we sat across
you. there was dirt under your
r nails and dark rings around
eyes. you asked me how finals
nodding and listening with
.. or care. or maybe apathy.
ur pockets as our livers sip slowly from
happy hour sangrias
i slid miniature bottles of tequila & rum across the table, then said you couldn't be
nds with us anymore. i had your christmas present in my purse. i was livid, and yelled,
again, she
won't let you
be friends with
us. when you
hugged us
goodbye/ why
did you smile?
what did i
miss

a. it's always tequila, a trifecta of tequila.
ids from movie theater photo booths dry
slipped a hand up my skirt. your mother was calling, then she called again. you
could feel my makeup run in the august heat. on the way home, you
you found me before picking up your bags. You said i was beautiful- i
called from the plane to say you landed. i heard your voice in
time the automatic doors flew open. i hadn't worn underwear that day. you
down in the passenger terminal at mccord. my skirt fluttered every
sweat collected at the crooks of my knees. i paced/sat down/paced/sat

again.

our espressos arrived and we paused.

out of the dark
& towards you
2500 miles
2500 miles
2500 miles
2500 miles
2500 miles
2500 miles
2500 miles
2500 miles
2500 miles
you sent a flashlight

a swirl of
ruffles
some light

my moth
you

enfolds me in her familiar id
i smell the aroma of coffee
-moon roast and something
and vanilla the fragrance of youth
on my mother's neck, accompanied
-rooted
expectant visitor. wrapped in overflow
ustastically in soft pastel floral i pull up the
my own as my mother decorates herself
in modest ancestral pearls
d burgundy pews became seats of transcendence
rough ornate stain glassed windows we
guised as matured wine from

when i learned i could
be a human being alone

it was raining. no. it was sunny this time. it was july. you held my hand on your favorite couch. steam was

i sat in a museum
in seattle

from the coffee cup in your other hand. your eyes wiggled now when you focused on an object/subject. you

the rain beat down
on the windows lights flickered

comes with age. i asked to hear your stories from the war again, knowing it would be the last. you smiled.

from the storm and i encountered
martha rosler and

pointed to a picture of me on your favorite coffee table and said i was your angel. the hearing aids you emp

kehinde wiley and
_____ and

whistled from your ears often. you told me the stories this time. i think, then attempted to rise to make brea

i was getting your texts
but i kept pushing them
back into my purse

your round belly was gone; you were swimming in your sweaters. your knees shook, even with braces. you h

are you
my
understudy father?

grandpa   that night with us, then died in september.   will you

fill the role

the smell of home burnt coffee lingering from the kitchen

when he inevitably

twenty year old dust dies on shelves that can no longer be

calls in sick?

i pay a stranger to touch me
reached you exist in my other childhood
and i'm reminded
again

i shake the hands

the could-have-been childhood—

of your colleagues

tepid sand between painted toes instead of pine needles

how it feels

you into those days we lived
with me. the margaritas

entangled in my hair, worn down flannels

to be human

about our shaking bodies,
we laid on the floor in ou

became your second skin until you traded them in

in possession
of a body

office. we wrote a poem to explai
what is/ protecting

for stiff hospital gowns.

it was noon on a wednesday. you took me
in a salt-rimmed existence. the margaritas
ping-ponged around our shaking bodies,
giggling. in darkness, we laid on the floor in ou
tiny campus office. we wrote a poem to explai
to capture/ to tell someone (maybe us) why
these events were happening/ were justifiabl

grandpa was
grandpa was
grandpa was
grandpa was

what the waves came
in and/ were justifiabl
keeping me
that moment. that was in may.
all. finally. we hadn't y

we met at the coffee shop. that was not a was
helens ave in tacoma. we saw was not an is
from you. there was dirt under was not an is
finger nails and dark was not an is
your eyes. you asked me how finals

i saw you last week. finally. we hadn't y
forgotten about it.

tequila, it's always tequila. a trifecta of tequila.
went, nodding and listening with
polaroids from movie theater photo booths dry
intent. or care. or maybe apathy.
in our pockets as our livers sip slowly from
happy hour sangrias

again.
again.

found me before picking up your bags. You said i was beautiful- i
you slid miniature bottles of tequila & rum across the table, then said you couldn't be
friends with us anymore. i had your christmas present in my purse. i was livid, and yelled,
then you said
i think, you just sat there and took it. our espressos arrived and we paused.
again, she
won't let you
be friends with
us. when you hugged us

out of the dark
& towards you
2500 miles
2500 miles
2500 miles
2500 miles
2500 miles
2500 miles
2500 miles
2500 miles
2500 miles

goodbye
from you, hugged us
a deep-rooted
led enthusiastically in soft pastel floral
my own as my mother decorates herself
in modest ancestral pearls
us up through ornate stain glassed windows we i
juice disguised as matured wine from

enfolds me in her familiar idyll
i smell the aroma of coffee
afternoon roast and something
and vanilla the fragrance of youth, a swirl of
my mother's neck, accompanied
expectant visitor. wrapped in overflo
i pull up the
you sent a flashlight

when i learned i could
be a human being alone

is raining. no. it was sunny this time. It was july. you held my hand on your favorite couch. steam was rising

i sat in a museum
in seattle

the coffee cup in your other hand. your eyes wiggled now when you focused on an object/subject. you said it

the rain beat down
on the windows lights flickered

nes with age. i asked to hear your stories from the war again, knowing it would be the last. you smiled. you

from the storm and i encountered
martha rosler and

ted to a picture of me on your favorite coffee table and said i was your angel. the hearing aids you employed

kehinde wiley and
_____ and

tled from your ears often. you told me the stories this time, i think, then attempted to rise to make breakfast.

i was getting your texts
but i kept pushing them
back into my purse

are you

und belly was gone. you were swimming in your sweaters. your knees shook, even with braces. you had a ful

my

understudy father?

grandpa.s that night with us, then died in september.   will you

the smell of home burnt coffee lingering from the kitchen

fill the role

twenty year old dust dies on shelves that can no longer be

when he inevitably

I pay a stranger to touch me
reached you exist in my other childhood
and i'm reminded
the could-have-been childhood—
again
tepid sand between painted toes instead of pine needles
how it feels
entangled in my hair, worn down flannels
to be human
became your second skin until you traded them in
in possession
for stiff hospital gowns.
of a body.

calls in sick?
i shake the hands
of your colleagues
you into those days we lived

grandpa was
grandpa was
grandpa was
grandpa was

it was noon on a wednesday. we made me
in a salt-rimmed existence. the margaritas
ping-ponged around our shaking bodies,
giggling. in darkness, we laid on the floor in our
tiny campus office. we wrote a poem to explain/
to capture/ to tell someone (maybe us) why
these events were happening
that moment. that was in may.
i saw you last week.
forgotten about it.

net at the coffee shop that is not a was
ns ave in tacoma. we saw was not an is
you. there was dirt under your was not an is
er nails and dark wings around was not an is
eyes. you asked me how finals

academ----ized stats
about our shaking bodies,
what is this telling me
in ending/ were justifiable at
keeping that
all of. finally. we hadn't yet

again.

la. it's always tequila. a trifecta of tequila.
nodding and listening with
olds from movie theater, photo booths dry
t. or care. or maybe apathy.
ur pockets as our livers sip slowly from
happy hour sangrias

slipped a hand up my skirt. your mother was calling, then she called again.
could feel my makeup run in the august heat. on the way home. you
you found me before picking up your bags. You said i was beautiful. i

u slid miniature bottles of tequila & rum across the table, then said you couldn't be

was livid, and yelled,

ends with us anymore. i had your christmas present in my purse. i

think, you just sat there and took it. our espressos arrived and we paused.

called from the plane to say you landed. i hadn't heard your phone in

again, she

time the automatic doors flew open. i hadn't worn underwear that day. you

won't let you
be friends with

down in the passenger terminal at mcchord. my skirt flaunted every

us. when you

sweat collected at the crooks of my knees. i paced/sat down/paced/sat

my mother

hugged us

out of the dark

black

goodbye, why
did you smile?
lingering
-rooted,
huslastically in soft pastel floral i pull up the
in modest ancestral pearls
ed burgundy pews became seats of transcendence
hrough ornate stain glassed windows we i
isguised as matured wine from

enfolds me in her familiar idyll
i smell the aroma of coffee
jasmine
afternoon roast and something
and vanilla the fragrance of youth
what did i
a swirl of
miss expectant visitor. wrapped in overflowed ruffles
my own as my mother decorates herself

& towards you
2500 miles
2500 miles
2500 miles
2500 miles
2500 miles
2500 miles
2500 miles
2500 miles
2500 miles
you sent a flashlight

dress
unzippe
curtsyin
down
my
waist
howling
at
the
half
quarter
moon

it was raining. no. it was sunny this time. it was july. you held my hand on your favorite couch. steam was r[ising]

when i learned i could
be a human being alone

from the coffee cup in your other hand. your eyes wiggled now when you focused on an object/subject. you s[aid]

i sat in a museum
in seattle

comes with age. i asked to hear your stories from the war again, knowing it would be the last. you smiled.

the rain beat down
on the windows lights flickered

pointed to a picture of me on your favorite coffee table and said i was your angel. the hearing aids you empl[oyed]

from the storm and i encountered
martha rosler and

are you
my

kehinde wiley and
_____ and

understudy father?

whistled from your ears often. you told me the stories this time, i think, then attempted to rise to make break[fast]

i was getting your texts
but i kept pushing them

will you
fill the role

our round belly was gone; you were swimming in your sweaters. your knees shook, even with braces. you ha[d]

back into my purse
grandpa[?] that night with us, then died in september.

when he inevitably
calls in sick?

the smell of home burnt coffee lingering from the kitchen
twenty year old dust dies on shelves that can no longer be
reached you exist in my other childhood
the could-have-been childhood—
tepid sand between painted toes instead of pine needles
entangled in my hair worn down flannels
became your second skin until you traded them in
for stiff hospital gowns.

i pay a stranger to touch me
and i'm reminded
how it feels
to be human
in possession
of a body.

i shake the hands
of your colleagues
you introduce me

grandpa was
grandpa was
grandpa was
grandpa was

it was noon on a wednesday. those memorized stats
in a salt-rimmed existence. the margaritas
ping-ponged around our shaking bodies,
giggling. in darkness, we laid on the floor in our
tiny campus office. we wrote a poem trying to
to capture/ to tell someone (maybe us) why
these events were happening while we were justifiable at
that moment. that was our
i saw you last week. finally. we hadn't yet
forgotten about it.

we met at the coffee shop that was not a was
helens ave in tacoma. we saw was not an is
from you. there was dirt under your was not an is
finger nails and dark rings around was not an is
your eyes. you asked me how finals
tequila. it's always tequila. a trifecta of tequila.
went, nodding and listening with
polaroids from movie theater photo booths dry
intent. or care. or maybe apathy.
in our pockets as our livers sip slowly from

again.

and a hand up my skirt. your mother was calling. then she called again.
would feel my makeup run in the august heat. on the way home. you
i found me before picking up your bags. You said i was beautiful. i

you slid miniature bottles of tequila & rum across the table, then said you couldn't be
friends with us anymore. i had your christmas present in my purse. i was livid, and yelled,
i think, you just sat there and took it. our espresso stained lips pointed at the moon in the telescope (you nodded)
and i tried to write something down. my fingers lacke[d]
then you said
again, she
won't let you
be friends with
us. when you
enfolds me in her familiar id

from you hugged us
goodbye? why
did you smile?
what did i
miss

out of the dark
& towards you

breathed deep. for awhile.

2500 miles
2500 miles
2500 miles
2500 miles
2500 miles
2500 miles
2500 miles
2500 miles

i watched jupiter's moons glimmer faintly through the
telescope. you asked if my hands were warm enough
to write yet. i nodded. the guide was circling
constellations with a laser than seemed to penetrate th[e]
darkness of our the universe. i turned to you and
whispered: don't you feel cosmically insignificant?
isn't it a beautiful feeling?

my mother
afternoon roast and something oldo
i smell the aroma of coffee
fingers and vanilla the fragrance of you
a deep-rooted my mother's neck, accompanied
miss expectant visitor. wrapped in overflo
ed enthusiastically in soft pastel floral i pull up the
my own as my mother decorates herself
in modest ancestral pearls
e tattered burgundy pews became seats of transcendence
s up through ornate stain glassed windows we i[n]
uice disguised as matured wine from

you sent a flashlight

In 1953, 27-year-old Henry Molaison [H.M. for short] went in for surgery to remove a small part of his brain. He had been diagnosed with epilepsy at a young age and suffered from seizures regularly. During surgery, Doctor Scoville removed H.M.'s amygdala and most of his hippocampus, which at that time shared a similar reputation with the appendix for being benign and a bit worthless.

As he recovered from surgery, his seizures were revealed to be gone, but so was his short-term memory. He could recall his life up until 27 but couldn't recall anything that occurred to him just fifteen minutes before.

In a medical breakthrough studied around the world, scientists and doctors finally discovered the significance the hippocampus has to the preservation of memory. Over the next fifty years, H.M. was studied extensively, from MRIs to memory tests, he was always happy and willing to help…once it was explained, again, why he was helping. His high I.Q. hadn't changed, and aspects of his personality remained the same, but H.M. was unable to lay down any new episodic memories.

Through a series of brainteasers it was revealed procedural memory, like learning a new language or riding a bike, remained. They had him write and draw designs while looking at a mirror to watch himself work. Without knowledge of how to accomplish the task, H.M. was able to perform the task that was asked of him, improving every time they had him try it. Semantic memory also remained present but extremely limited, allowing him to pick up new facts or statistics about pop culture or politics on a small scale.

When he died in 2008, there was a long line of individuals and organizations who wanted his brain for scientific research. Streaming live from the University of California, San Diego campus, thousands of people watched the 54-hour dissection of H.M.'s brain. Scientists continue to study his brain and acknowledge his case as one of the biggest neuro breakthroughs for science and memory.

Up to his death he had to be re-introduced to others and re-introduced to himself daily. Expecting to see his 27-year-old self in the mirror, he would have to be consoled when he saw an old man staring back at him.

*

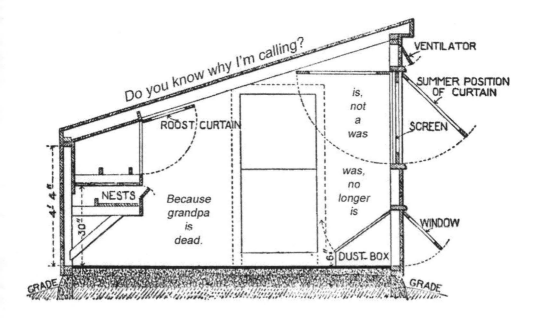

In the late 19th century, Sigmund Freud began treating female patients who were diagnosed as 'hysterical.' Through a series of hypnosis and touch therapy, Freud uncovered unconscious memories of trauma that the patients couldn't recall in their waking moments. He considered his investigations like unlocking a door of repressed memories. Lying on worn couches, women laid their unconscious minds bare for Freud to prod around in. He was the first individual to connect how trauma affects our minds and bodies. After some losses and some successes, Freud moved away from touch therapy and hypnosis in an effort to understand *why* memories are buried rather than *what* is buried.

John Locke, a 19th century philosopher, looked at memory as the blueprints of our identity. He believed our memories and experiences helped build character and changed the way we choose to behave throughout life. He disliked the practice of repeated memorization, arguing that the self will naturally remember what it deems necessary and important. He viewed memory as a storehouse, a building to hoard ideas, waiting for a particular moment in time to revive certain memories. "They are actually nowhere, but only there is an ability in the mind, when it will, to revive them again; and as it were paint them anew on itself."

"You should talk to me."

"About what, Mom?"

"Everything? Anything? I would take anything at this point."

"There's nothing to share. I'm good."

"I hope you share more with your therapist then. That relationship couldn't have been easy to deal with, not to mention navigating the eating d—"

"Mom," I stop her. "I'm good. Promise."

She had picked me up from the rehab facility forty-five minutes ago and I was already thinking about what injuries I might sustain from jumping out of her moving vehicle.

She studies me at the dinner table and I can almost see her cataloging everything I eat, night after night, nodding at random moments while chewing.

My mother recommends I see a therapist when my second series of migraines clusters the month of March.

APRIL

MAY

JUNE—

The tension headaches increase in frequency—the throbbing in my shoulders, the ache down my calves. My psychiatrist, Dr. Clark, is hitting a wall with me. I enjoy sitting in silence with her in that tiny room, every wall lined with books, but I don't imagine she enjoys the silence like I do. I picked up on her irritated tics early on—a pen tapping lightly against her thigh; a furtive glance to the clock; jotting down a note after a long stretch of quiet. I couldn't see her session notes but I'm sure scribbled somewhere on her legal notepad were notes such as "aversion to vulnerability" or "stubbornness a major characteristic flaw." We talk about everything, sometimes, except for what we need to talk about.

She recommends massage therapy to tackle the physical manifestations of stress in my body, thinking it might be an avenue to open the psychological manifestations she says I'm currently unable or unwilling to share.

*

I start seeing a masseuse bi-monthly. She's a close friend. "Shit.

You have a ton of knots in your body."

"I know."

"Like… a minefield of knots."

"I get it."

She turns on an instrumental and works the lavender oil into my skin in circles:

clockwise

rubbing

clockwise

kneading

rubbingkneadingrubbingkneading

She lightly works a few knots at a time; conjoined knots. Knots plotting.

"There are stretches I'd recommend to help prevent this kind of damage, and…"

2009- the BBQ is sizzling
burning the burgers
but you don't care

Boyfriend, H

that whiskey on
your breath again
more often than
mouth wash

you stand
closer to me
and

I think about the last time
I actually saw one of our
neighbors
near the
farm

the dog
paces as
you

chug a beer fist high yelling

who the fuck are you fucking

who the fuck are you fucking

who the fuck are you fucking

"Did you nod off?"

The stereo is already on track 10. The session clock has ten till.

My body is oiled and cool. Lavender fills my pores but I feel worse. She rinses her hands methodically—down to elbows and under fingernails.

"These knots I worked out will now allow more blood to flow in the previously cramped muscles. You'll be in pain for a bit but it'll fade eventually."

"How are the massages going?" My mom asks, flipping through the mail on her front coffee table.

"They're going." My mom purses her lips. I don't want to tell her about where my mind wanders during my sessions or how painful the appointments are. I reach down idly and run my fingers along my left calf, realizing with relief one of the bigger knots has disappeared.

"And your follow up appointments with Dr. Clark?"

"Also happening still. I wouldn't skip them."

"I wasn't insinuating you were skipping, I was wondering if you were talking to her yet."

"Well, sure. She says hello. I say hello. It's been grand so far." She drops the mail down and shoots me a look.

"You know what I mean. You're living here at home now, which I'm fine with, of course, but I expect a certain level of respect. Do you think I haven't gone through anything like this at one point? Why won't you just talk to me about it if you won't talk to others?" I chew on my lip but meet her gaze.

"There isn't much to talk about. I'm feeling better." Lying seems to be what I do best these days.

*

I book another appointment with my masseuse.

She tells me massage and acupuncture hones in on essential pressure points—the muscle map of my body. She tells me the knots under my shoulder blades and up my neck are stretching my muscles like a rubber band. My wilted posture is changing the shape. My body has acclimated to tension.
She tells me:

pressure & release

pressure & release

pressure & release

I ask her just to get rid of them.

Laying on the table face down, she twists my arm back, scooping fingers under the blade. She rubs around a knot, circling it, applying pressure until it's unbearable.

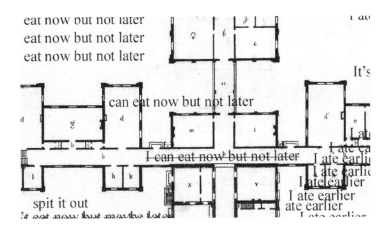

I squeeze my eyes shut. Let out a gasp from deep in my lungs. She asks if the pressure is too much.

"Keep going."

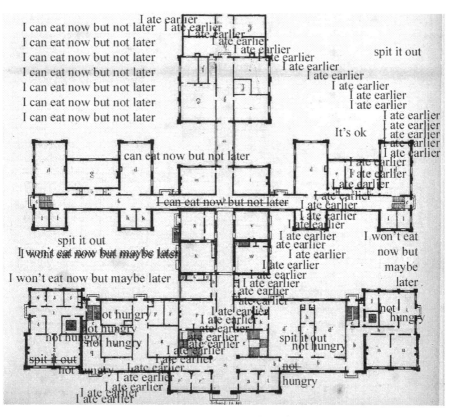

I ask if it's gone yet. She shrugs and hands me a glass of water.

"Time to flush the toxins."

I schedule a follow up for Friday, even though she doesn't recommend this frequency. As she washes the oil from her hands she says over her shoulder: "You get so quiet during your appointments. Most of my clients like to talk—about their jobs, their spouses, whatever. You don't seem inclined to do that."

"Do I need to talk?"

"I don't know," she says, finally meeting my glance. "Do you?" I look over at the massage table, the donut-shaped hole where my face just lay.

"It's weird, but I don't feel anxious when I come here. Or

afraid. I can just be for a bit." It's been a while since I found a space that affords me that liberty. I find something in the quiet.

She nods as she finishes drying her hands. "Some of my clients discover an emotional release in addition to their physical release post-massage—many even cry when it happens." I stare at her blankly.

"I'm just sayin, if you need to cry, do it. I've been friends with you for over a decade now and I've never seen you burst."

Looking across the table from Dr. Clark, I readjust my skirt.

She smiles.

"How is your mother?"

"Prodding more and more often."

"Have you opened up to her these past few months?" No.

"She knows what happened to me."

"And your massage therapy sessions?" My eyebrows furrow in silence. "I'm taking it not well?"

"No," I begin, "they're going well. Some of my knots are gone and my tension headaches aren't occurring as often. I've even been sleeping longer through the nights."

"That's excellent progress." She turns a page in her notebook and scribbles something else. "Have you been keeping up with your food diary?" I pull it out of my bag and hand it over the desk to her. She studies a few pages closely, flips a few more pages and analyzes another note. "Looks like you've been eating pretty consistently. Are you experiencing any feelings of remorse post-meals?" Yes.

"No."

Scribble.

"Do you think you're at a point now where you're ready to talk about the abuse?"

I'm only aware of my knuckles tightening around the arms of the chair. The session clock dings on her desk, and I exhale. She looks up, capturing an image of my relief, and jots it down.

*

I ask my masseuse friend to focus on specific pressure points this time, not knowing what the process will dredge up, but knowing it is necessary to eliminate these moments from my body. I want to feel healthy again. I want to be loved and have the capacity to love others. I want to try to live in the shape of my body. Whatever shape that may take. I want to purge and renew. I want to be possessed, again, by the feeling of being alive—in excitement, in desire, in elation, in confusion, in pain and in love.

She works a knot that has been lingering in my thighs. Oil slicks and shines on her fingertips. I grimace as her fingertips graze stretchmarks but swiftly she moves, glistening and propelled by coconut oil. A quick flinch jolts from me involuntarily as she zeroes in on the knot. She shoots me a look, checking in on my pain tolerance. I nod.

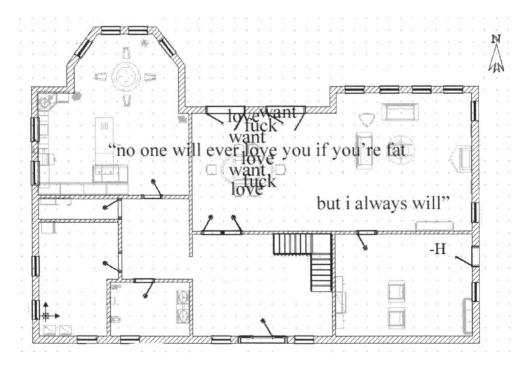

She reapplies oil to her palms, smearing it back and forth to warm the liquid before applying it to my skin.

She runs two fingers along both sides of my spine and fans out—looking for more knots hiding in between muscles. Finding one in my lower back, she murmurs: "This one might hurt a bit more." I link my fingers together under the table bracing myself, wondering, on this increasing scale of pain, when I would break. If I would.

She has me lean forward, inhaling the aroma therapy mix from her palms.

One deep breath in, one out. One deep breath in, one out.

One more deep breath in, one out.

Thirty minutes into my appointment she glides up to the muscles that span my shoulders. I wonder if she saved this for last. She works one under my right shoulder blade—

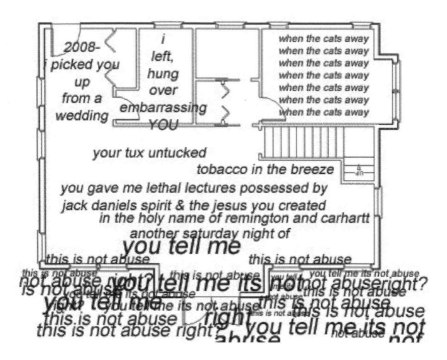

Moving, she trains her grip on a knot at the base of my neck. She grumbles from behind me: "This is a tough one. Damn." Her fingers work in circles, applying more pressure than I am accustomed to. I grip the legs of the table and hold my breath until I see stars.

"You good?" I nod quickly.

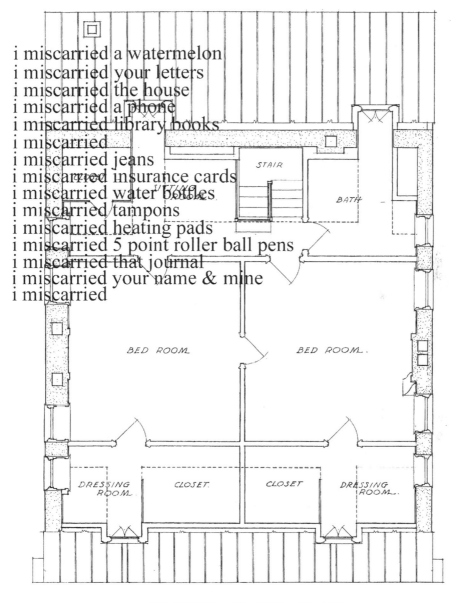

i miscarried a watermelon
i miscarried your letters
i miscarried the house
i miscarried a phone
i miscarried library books
i miscarried
i miscarried jeans
i miscarried insurance cards
i miscarried water bottles
i miscarried tampons
i miscarried heating pads
i miscarried 5 point roller ball pens
i miscarried that journal
i miscarried your name & mine
i miscarried

STAIR

BATH

BED ROOM

BED ROOM

DRESSING ROOM

CLOSET

CLOSET

DRESSING ROOM

SECOND FLOOR PLAN

D EVAN WALL - DEL

A sharp exhale escapes my lips as pain shoots through my body, rippling from my thighs—lower back—arms—shoulder blades—echoing out, each ripple intensifying.

The arch of my neck recoils in response. My vision tunnels and my eyes burst. She pauses the session clock and dims the lights. Her motions feel choreographed, like this response is completely normal. Like she was expecting this outcome. I fight the urge to stifle the crying, choosing to embrace the uncomfortable abnormality I had become. Hesitantly she places her palm on my naked back, small circled pats orbiting my shoulders.

"I don't know what to say," I breathe, hearing something in my voice between the sobs I don't recognize. These words by themselves meant nothing, but strung together and filtered through my body, mixing with the pain and shock of release, I knew what it was: It was the sound of admission. I recognized sadness; had tasted denial on my tongue for months, mixed with saliva and stomach acid. But my muscles held guilt; held every skipped meal; held every "I love you/I hate you"; every moment of betrayal I thought I had dealt with. I still feel the indentation of his fingerprints through dead skin on my body. For years my body belonged to his body—my hair, my tongue, the valley between my hips, the freckle behind my knee—his for occasional devotion, for revision, for relief, for perception, for sound and silence, for abuse. At this moment as tears escape me and the release still flows through newly freed muscles, I feel this body is mine again.

*

I never visited my dad that day in the hospital. I want to believe I did.

I should have, but I didn't. I was in a relationship with H, a man who told me I needed to come home every day straight after work. If I wasn't prompt, he'd start drinking early. With the threat constantly looming over me from the blare of the morning alarm, I left my dad in a hospital room and went home to a man who loved to hate me.

I've stared down at empty pages more often that I'd like to admit. I'd reach back in my body, looking for words, the potentiality of sentences, but finding only visuals. Accessing memories in my body shook me.

A moment of trauma would fire—I'd probe every corner of it to document and manipulate, push through the space and expand it to find what I missed from before. I walked through every memory with my back to the boundaries of the space I explored, keeping my distance from H and from falling back into those moments of time. But my neck would throb with heat, glistening. My pupils dilated and my pulse hummed high in my ears. As if imagining him would summon him.

I'd burn down the houses I shared with him if it meant exorcising every memory of mine he possesses.

One evening I drove out to the country town I shared with him, not sure what I was looking for. There's a quiet hum of grasshoppers over this town. Pickup truck after pickup truck line the bars in the center of town like tiles. In the summers you could always hear cows bellowing one or two farms over; manure and fresh cut hay on the breeze.

I was high on adrenaline; I chewed on mints to keep my teeth from grinding. My body fought every turn I made through town, begging me to turn around, come to my senses and run. Driving by the places that once haunted me, I saw his familiar shadow under vibrating fluorescent lights, enveloped in smoke, outside that same old bar.

The first time H coerced me into having sex he said it was for love. He said I should do it before he finds someone else. He said he fantasized about my thick thighs wrapped around him; tugging on my long hair. He wasn't gentle. He took what he saw was his and left the room. I reached down and blood slipped between my fingertips. I texted my best friend, the chat box littered with exclamation points, hiding what should have been question marks. I lived as an exclamation point when others asked about me and my life with him, never revealing the question mark that my body really was.

I had given it once—therefore my body existed for his taking. And he did.

When I left him, my imagination spun tales—fantastical and wild. I imagined he'd fled or been shamed into hiding; drank himself to death; ran off a Carbonado cliff with bourbon between his legs; became aware of the human being that he was. In every figment I created, he no longer had a corporeal body.

DIGESTIVE: on Friday nights you & I went to dinner in the small hick town where we lived. We'd meet your friends there & the evening would tip, licked by liquor, & you'd escape to the bar down the hall & around the corner. You'd go knowing I wasn't old enough to follow. A green-eyed doe trained to sit & obey. My intestines knotted—grew intimate with the tension of Friday nights. I crushed tums between teeth to balance the jitters. The taste on my tongue was metallic.

CIRCULATORY: irregular palpitations beat through a stethoscope, the doctor's question lingered in her furrowed brow: "what stresses exist in your daily life?"

INTEGUMENTARY: I pick at my cuticles until they bleed. Old habit rising from raised voices. And whiskey, of course. I chew on broken nails to prevent me from speaking. The hair on my arms prick & sway; crescent-shaped depressions in my palms made the shape of my body.

MUSCULAR: shoulders slump & muscles contract—tendons tense & flex; reactive. My knuckles knew the memory of curling into a pillow; the balance needed to demonstrate pleasure vs. fear.

REPRODUCTIVE: Friday night rewards—sour whiskey & coke on my throat, I compiled grocery lists in my head while you were inside me, eager, knuckles deep, sightseeing without a map of my body. Headlights passed by the window & set the room on fire. You didn't mind the chafing like I did, but you also didn't care.

ENDOCRINE: My menstrual blood set you off, knowing it bewitched me; replenished the power to my senses—a natural repellant to your good ol' country boy.

I'd let it run wild between thick thighs, savor in the space it created apart from you—

But I lived & breathed by the ten commandments of you because you told me to. If you'd raised your hand high, to strike or condemn, ruling menstruation a sin I would have plugged it up & prayed god to take the power from my undeserving ovaries.

SKELETAL: cartilage now pops when I get down on my knees. I was just crumpled bones in a moonlit room.

Before I went to sleep, I'd whisper: am I even still a human being?

RESPIRATORY: I held my breath for five years—followed by a six-month exhale that hurricaned through my blood & baptized my body.

NERVOUS: I've hollowed out my adrenal glands with a dirty spoon—wrung 'em & hung 'em out to dry—but that splash of spirits on your tongue or the tongues of others calls for shots of endorphins, tranquilizing senses while an overworked homeostasis clocks in & out and in & out, working nights & weekends.

LYMPHATIC: flushing you was a five-year endeavor—cayenne pepper and liquid diets, night sweats & marathon retching, eliminated alcohol, ate seaweed & dandelion root, vinyasa'd under the moon, exfoliated dead skin, leaving you in supermarkets & alleyways, submerged myself in sex, cored myself like an apple & built myself back up, bone by bone.

As we age, neurons fire less often while our cerebral engine loses shape and elasticity. Cognitive disruption begins to occur as blood flow to the frontal and temporal lobes slows, missing connections with synapses that are struggling to connect. The overall lobe volume of our brain shrinks as neurological processes prioritize what's more important: remembering to mail our bills or retaining that second language we've let slip.

Gradual memory loss is expected, significant memory loss is a symptom. In the beginning it's hard to notice—missing a deadline, forgetting a family dinner—before it unfolds into missing your exit home and forgetting your spouse's name. Dementia takes shape in many forms, most recognizably as Alzheimer's. The cause of the disease is still unknown, but health, environment, and genetics all play a factor.

Alzheimer's disease damages and, eventually, kills healthy nerve cells in your brain, ruining the synaptic connections irreparably. Our frontal cortex may call upon a memory but discovers the hippocampus has already taken a seat on the bench.

Doctors often measure the shrinkage occurring in a patient's temporal or parietal lobes to indicate the loss of nerve cells, the primary test that diagnoses the disease. Sometimes they run basic short-term memory tests. Rarely do they draw blood or spinal fluid in an attempt to rule out other medical conditions. Typically, within a year of an AD diagnosis, the brain shrinks severely and begins to affect not only memory, but behavioral and cognitive functions. No longer will you be able to prioritize your own life properly, or even recognize that you're encountering issues making decisions on your own.

Occasionally doctors will prescribe supplements containing Acetylcholine (ACh), a chemical produced naturally in your brain that strengthens learning and memory. Drugs containing ACh could potentially help improve memory, but it's merely a band-aid.

You'll tell the same stories over and over again, the ones you actually remember, as your family and friends nod and smile. Knowingly. You leave the stove on. You let your talents lapse. You forget family traditions. You forget that you are forgetting.

*

Don't forget, Nicole is coming to visit next week.

She is? That's wonderful.

*

Don't forget, Nicole is coming to visit in a few days.

She is? OK.

*

Don't forget, Nicole will be here in two days. Who?

Your granddaughter.

Oh yes. It'll be so good to see her.

*

Don't forget, Nicole will be at our house tomorrow around 9 a.m.

She's visiting? What a lovely surprise.

FALSIFY.

My dad lies in a hospital bed, out of breath, his voice stolen by illness. The teal hospital gown looks foreign on his large body. The hospital room is barren apart from the TV and miscellaneous anxiety-inducing medical equipment. He misses his dogs. He misses his lighthouse figurines. He misses his big screen TV.

"This room gets *horrible* reception," he whispers, "I have a DVR at home full of my shows I'm missing." I nod. The room doesn't even have a window—anything I can stare out of to avoid eye contact. An open nothingness I can let my eyes relax into, blurring the reality in front of me.

"They keep giving me turkey sandwiches that taste days old." I offer to bring him some of his favorites, our family pasta dish, concocting a plan to smuggle it in. He shrugs.

My younger brother slumps his shoulders, his large frame wilting and weak, flipping through channels for dad. The Big Bang Theory appears on the screen and my dad's laugh escapes his lungs in struggled rasps—"this show is so funny; I always get a kick out of it."

The doctor knocks quickly and my brother mutes the television. In a lengthy summary filled with medical terms and multiple options, as if he was being paid per word, the doctor inquires about testing for severe sleep apnea as a last resort. A 'Hail Mary' of sorts to save his life.

The overnight test is scheduled. The sleeping equipment ordered. My dad smiles. Hopelessly.

Self-storage industry leaders indicate units are needed for four primary reasons: dislocation, divorce, downsizing, and death. The bright orange brochure brags about 142 million square feet of space for sale nationwide.

I'm surrounded by boxes labeled "FRAGILE! Memories" or "FRAGILE! Pictures & picture frames."

I've sifted through every box, every closet, every cubby of this house, encountering objects linked to memories, then making the decision of what stays and what goes.

People rent storage units for their overflow, or when they're in a state of transition. $88 a month to store your memories and enchanted objects. Night after night I've driven past rows of crowded units, some with contents bursting, spilling out on the concrete, demanding to be acknowledged. We pack our own unit to the roof trusting in Public Storage to keep it safe for us.

Half my books won't see daylight for six months. My wedding pictures with R crowd each other in misshapen boxes. Dust settles on storage bins and time becomes irrelevant in that 8-foot by 10-foot space.

I stop by late one night to inhale our old sheets, eager to smell our previous home, but discover that the cheap fibers have already consumed the musty nothingness of the unit. It's a lonely smell.

My mother and her brother kept a few storage units for nearly a decade, each one overflowing with wooden craft projects and military paperwork that belonged to their dad. Every time we unhooked the lock and rolled the door open, the smell of worn leather and dust enveloped us, and the fragrant sugary odor he sprayed to hide his smoking habit.

The smell of this grandpa is the only thing I remember about him. I would sit in his lap, inhaling deeply from collars of flannel, letting a busy world settle for a bit.

My mom kept him alive, contained in units that continued to emanate his scent.

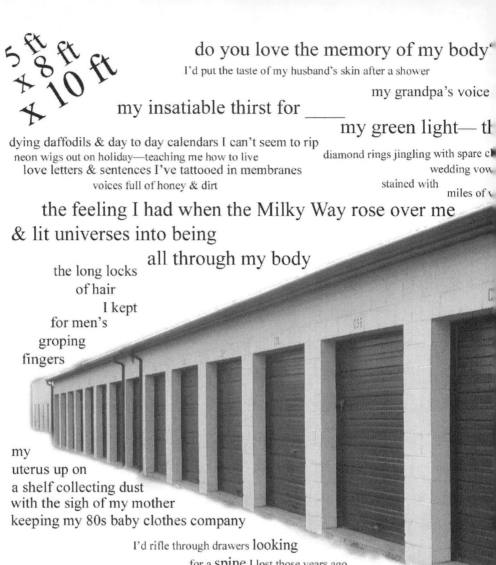

5 ft x 8 ft x 10 ft

do you love the memory of my body'
I'd put the taste of my husband's skin after a shower

my grandpa's voice

my insatiable thirst for _____

my green light— th

dying daffodils & day to day calendars I can't seem to rip
neon wigs out on holiday—teaching me how to live
love letters & sentences I've tattooed in membranes
voices full of honey & dirt

diamond rings jingling with spare ch
wedding vow
stained with
miles of v

the feeling I had when the Milky Way rose over me
& lit universes into being
all through my body

the long locks
of hair
I kept
for men's
groping
fingers

my
uterus up on
a shelf collecting dust
with the sigh of my mother
keeping my 80s baby clothes company

I'd rifle through drawers looking
for a spine I lost those years ago
ground to a powder
ingested & spit out with tobacco

I'd file away every conversation containing "why" or "you"
lies like arsenic

lost & _____:
oman
may-
november
2011
herat
november
2012-
july
2013
bagram
february-
october
2014
saudi arabia
february-
may
2016

but

I'd p

I'd pack the incessant pounding at every
love utterance:

trembling knees
moist palms
dilated pupils
that contagious shiver
so I could try them on   every friday night
over and over
over and over
hands grazing shoulders
like a slip under a dress

other enchanted object?

d in voicemails

eding horizon

ins

eployment you and me
    encased in the back
      clad in bubble wrap——

time before you learned
      to live without home
       and I learned I could live

          without you

3 P.M. PHONE CONVERSATION WITH DAD:

DAD: Your brother brought the kids over for Halloween so they could trick or treat at my house. Their costumes were pretty cute.

ME: That's cool they stopped by your house.

DAD: *HAHAHA* Your niece must have locked my front door on her way out because I was standing on the porch smoking—

ME: Like you do.

DAD: Yeah, anyway—so they pack up the grandkids and get them buckled up, and just as they're driving away I realize I'm locked out of my house! I ran down my driveway, without shoes, yelling at them to come back so your brother can help me back in.

ME: Did they hear you?

DAD: Oh yeah, they did. Your brother hopped the fence and luckily I had left the back door open for the dogs. *HAHAHA* Can you imagine if they hadn't heard me? She may be 3 but I'm going to give her a hard time for locking grandpa out of his house.

6 P.M. DINNER CONVERSATION WITH DAD:

DAD: you'll never guess what   did the other day. *HAHAHA* She must have locked my front door on her way out on Halloween (they stopped by to trick or treat) because I was standing on the porch smoking and just as they're driving away I realize I'm locked out of my house! I ran down my driveway waving and hollering at them to come back *HAHAHA* Your brother hopped the fence and luckily I had left the back door open for the dogs.

ME: DAD— you just told me this story on the phone less than four hours ago.

DAD: I did?

ME: Yes.

DAD: Gonna take away my keys next?

Last week, my dad repeated the same story to me twice within a span of four hours. He told me once on the phone, then told me every detail again over dinner—every laugh the same, his eyes lit with expression, the joy that fills your body the first time you share a memory with someone else.

After my grandpa died, my grandma's mental capacity deteriorated in brief but permanent occurrences. Now on a limited income, my aunts seized her checkbook to prevent her from giving her mortgage money away to charity again. They removed the Home Shopping Network from her speed dial and cancelled the rip-off juice diet subscription she swore by. At Christmas and on birthdays we have to mail back or cancel the checks she sends. She adjusts to life signing checks that no longer share the heading with my grandpa's name.

One night she walked miles to the grocery store alone in Southern California. My aunt received a phone call from a store employee asking for someone to pick her up. She was frantic and confused and couldn't locate her cell phone. Upon arrival, my aunt found the cell phone in my grandma's purse. They took her car keys from her the next day.

Yesterday at dinner my dad said she repeated the same story about my grandpa four times in the span of one evening

without ever acknowledging she had done it. Aunts, daughters, cousins, grandchildren there as witness. My dad remained quiet after telling us, like briefing an unrelated news story, but I could hear _____ get caught in his vocal cords.

*

My dad peers in the short order window of our favorite greasy diner on Kent-Kangley and, leaning down on elbows, I watch him expel cigarette smoke in the cold night air through his wrinkled mustache. He lets a dad joke or two out. Humor is his safety net to connect with other people. My younger brother's small feet barely scuff the floor mats; my pre-teen body in the front seat is a shape trying to be another shape.

He orders more than we need:

"Do we need milkshakes? We need milkshakes," he says to them. The diner sign is always half lit and tagged with graffiti. The teenager hands him the order ticket through the window, and as ritual, he folds it and keeps it secure in his t-shirt pocket behind his pack of cigarettes.

Fries and milkshakes out of mind, our only goal is to guess the number on the order ticket. Like Bingo without the prize, we shout out numbers and he replies with whimsy like our Saturday morning cartoon characters.

There is no prize. We still get to eat the contents of grease-stained bags. It's playing this game with him, sharing this time untouched by our mother that make this spontaneous junk food run worth _____. These nights with his kids heading to restaurants reminiscent of California diners of his youth [I think] make these setting Washington nights more bearable.

Here, sitting in the car with my 60-year-old dad, I wonder how long it'll be before he forgets this memory.

Or when I will.

"Even the act of deliberate destruction
is a memorial
to the thing
it is designed
to destroy."
–Edward Hollis
The Memory Palace: A Book of Lost Interiors

i have a pattern
for loving men
who drink
deep

mouths always
open,
ready to consume
the world

i flay myself
wide enough
to let them
saturate my cells
with bourbon

so i
can never
forget

MANIPULATE.
[2010: H]

Thursday afternoon. 4 p.m.

The farmhouse is quiet. I beat him home from work.

I could run this time—
My pulse palpitates as I think about how quickly I
could pack up what's mine.

The bathroom would be easy—grab the load of
laundry from the night before. My mom could give
me another toothbrush.
I can leave the Ross variety kitchenware, dirty in the
sink.

The bedroom—we shared a twin and didn't sleep on
sheets.

I could snatch clothes by the hangers—sweaters,
bras, dresses uprooted, fainting in my arms

I'd crawl on worn knees to clear out the attic—

pupils dilated, humming in my ears, high on the
thought of leaving.

I would need a whole day. I could take tomorrow off,
or next Friday.

I think about stripping the framed pictures from the
shelves
but rocks kick up the driveway
followed by the roar of an off-road muffler.

*

Thursday afternoon. 4 p.m.

The farmhouse is quiet. I beat him home from work.

My pulse palpitates as I think about how quickly I could pack up what's mine.

The bathroom would be easy—grab the load of laundry from the night before. Discard his hickories and long johns on dirty tiles. My mom could give me another toothbrush.
I can leave the Ross variety kitchenware, dirty in the sink. [but maybe I should wash them first?]

The bedroom—we shared a twin and didn't sleep on sheets. We never had sheets.
At night we could hear farm mice racing back & forth

I could snatch clothes by the hangers—sweaters, bras, dresses uprooted, fainting in my arms
A trail of socks to the car

I'd crawl on worn knees to clear out the attic—an asylum of 200 square feet

pupils dilated, humming in my ears, high on the thought of leaving.

I would need a whole day. I could take tomorrow off, or next Friday. That's what I'll do. I'll take next Friday off.

I think about stripping the framed pictures from the shelves
Cutting his body out—
but rocks kick up the driveway
followed by the roar of an off-road muffler.

*

Thursday afternoon. 4 p.m.

The farmhouse is quiet. I beat him home from work.

My pulse palpitates as I think about how quickly I could pack up what's mine.

The bathroom would be easy—grab the load of laundry from the night before. Discard his hickories and long johns on dirty tiles. My mom could give me another toothbrush.
I can leave the Ross variety kitchenware, dirty in the sink.
An army of beer cans crowd the stove, drained & defeated.

Mental notes I collected detail what movies are his & what are mine; what furniture is his & what is mine; what memories are his & what are mine.

The bedroom—we shared a twin and didn't sleep on sheets. We never had sheets.
At night we could hear farm mice racing back & forth while he was inside of me

I could snatch clothes by the hangers—sweaters, bras, dresses uprooted, fainting in my arms
A trail of socks to the car

I'd crawl on worn knees to clear out the attic—an asylum of 200 square feet
books stacked collecting webbing and rodent droppings

pupils dilated, humming in my ears, high on the thought of leaving.

I would need a whole day. I'll take next Friday off. Would I need help? Can I ask for help?

I think about stripping the framed pictures from the shelves
Cutting his body out—[*can I ever cut his body out?*]
but rocks kick up the driveway
followed by the roar of an off-road muffler.

*

Thursday afternoon. 4 p.m.

The farmhouse is quiet. I beat him home from work again.

My pulse palpitates as I think about how quickly I could pack up what's mine.

The bathroom would be easy—grab the load of laundry from the night before. Discard his hickories and long johns on dirty tiles. Sweep makeup and tampons and razors into Safeway bags. My mom could give me another toothbrush.
I can leave the Ross variety kitchenware, dirty in the sink.
An army of beer cans crowd the stove, drained & defeated, from last Friday. Flies circle the used tinfoil & tongs left to rot. Steaks marinating in the fridge next to my coffee creamer are waiting for their Friday night debut. Empty glass bottles clink a celebration in the recycling bin.

In the living room, mental notes I collected detail what movies are his & what are mine; what furniture is his & what is mine; what memories are his & what are mine. The loveseat can stay; the smell of Jim Beam breeds in its fibers.

The bedroom—we shared a twin and didn't sleep on sheets. We never had sheets.
At night we could hear farm mice racing back & forth while he was inside of me
as I watched the digital clock blink

I could snatch clothes by the hangers—sweaters, bras, dresses uprooted, fainting in my arms
A trail of socks to the car
[maybe I'd leave the wardrobe & start over?]

I'd crawl on bruised hands & worn knees to clear out
the attic—an asylum of 200 square feet
books stacked collecting webbing and rodent
droppings

pupils dilated, humming in my ears, high on the
thought of leaving. Of finally leaving.

I would need a whole day.

but
maybe I could stay—
maybe I should stay—

I think about stripping the framed pictures from the
shelves
Cutting his body out—[*can I ever cut his body out?*]
but rocks kick up the driveway
followed by the roar of an off-road muffler.

*

Thursday afternoon. 4 p.m.

The farmhouse is quiet. I beat him home from work again.

My pulse palpitates as I think about how quickly I could pack up what's left of mine.

The bathroom would be easy—grab the load of laundry from the night before. Discard his hickories and long johns on dirty tiles. Sweep makeup and tampons and razors into Safeway bags. My mom would give me another toothbrush.

I can leave the Ross variety kitchenware, dirty in the sink, keeping the broken mason jars company.
An army of beer cans crowd the stove, drained & defeated, from another Friday. Flies circle the used tinfoil & tongs left to rot. A steak marinates in the fridge next to my coffee creamer waiting for its Friday night debut. Empty glass bottles clink a celebration in the recycling bin.

In the living room—
the loveseat can stay; the smell of Jim Beam breeds in its fibers.
He'll burn the bookshelf. A sacrificial offering for his weekly bonfire.

The bedroom—we shared a twin and didn't sleep on sheets. We never had sheets.
At night we could hear farm mice racing back & forth while he was inside of me
chew & liquor on his tongue
a glass of Jim Beam sweats on the nightstand
as I watched the digital clock blink & blink & blink
another night of using my body as a lure, trading sex for sobriety

I could snatch clothes by the hangers—sweaters,
bras, dresses uprooted, fainting in my arms
A trail of socks to the car
[*maybe I'd leave the wardrobe & start over?*]

I'd crawl on bruised hands & worn knees to clear out
the attic—

books stacked collecting webbing and rodent
droppings

pupils dilated, humming in my ears, high on the
thought of leaving. Of finally leaving.

I would need a whole day.

I think about stripping the framed pictures from the
shelves
Cutting his body out—[*can I ever cut his body out?*
Can his body ever not be a part of my body?]
but rocks kick up the driveway
followed by the roar of an off-road muffler.

*

Thursday afternoon. 4p.m.

The farmhouse is quiet.

My pulse palpitates as I quickly pack up what's mine.

The bathroom was easy—grabbed the load of laundry
from the night before. Discarded hickories and long
johns on dirty tiles. Swept makeup and tampons and
razors into Safeway bags.

I left the Ross variety kitchenware, dirty in the sink.
An army of beer cans crowd the stove, drained &
defeated, from the last Friday.

In the living room—
the loveseat stayed. the couch stayed. the bookcase
stayed.

The bedroom—
I snatched clothes by the hangers—sweaters, bras,
dresses uprooted, fainting in my arms
A trail of socks to the car
the trunk an open mouth—ready for more

I crawled on hands & knees to clear out the attic—
freed books from webbing and rodent droppings

pupils dilated, humming in my ears, high on the act
of leaving. Of finally leaving.

I needed a whole day off. I took a whole day off.

I stripped the framed pictures from the shelves
cutting his body out
before rocks ever kick up the driveway.

can I ever cut him out?

can I
ever

you must
change this—
you must
you must
you must
you must
you must
you must
you must
you must
you must
you must
turn it over
you must
you must
you must
you must
you must
you must
you must
you must

MEMORY

ENTITLEMENT.

DAD: I saw on Instagram you posted a book you were recently published in.

ME: Yes, recently. It was on the shelves at Powell's.

DAD: It's a book about survivors.

DAD: I saw on Instagram you posted a book you were recently published in.

ME: Yes, recently. It was on the shelves at Powell's.

DAD: It's a book about survivors.

christmas eve 2008— [H]

i can't say i had a ~~boyfriend/lover~~ but your body was a misery my body craved.

you pinched my nipples hard & told me i was never on a pedestal but could work my way up,

my hunger for punishment you'd never seen before.

ME: Yes.

ME: Yes.

DAD: are you one of those

survivors?

DAD: are you one of those

survivors?

june 2010: [H] your voice rattled windows as your body exclaimed "WHO THE FUCK ARE YOU FUCKING" over and over and over and i wondered who i was and if there was anything left of me for you to consume. licking your lips i listened when you said you'd fuck the lesbian out of me

in a world you couldn't imagine a/this woman being repulsed by the body you made built with johnny's, jack & PBR

those days i took bites of the midnight moon with thegirls to keep your hands offme

i didn't let you in

ME: Yes.

ME: Yes.

DAD: When was that?

DAD: When was that?

how do i tell you this wasn't
an isolated incident?

DAD: Does your mom
know?

DAD: Does your mom
know?

you made me love you

what was it about you

you made me love you

what was it about you

you made me love you

what was it about you

you made me love you

what was it about you

this was the first man i let in

DAD: Was it at a party or
something?

DAD: Was it at a party or
something?

*2006 [H] locked in a
stranger's bathroom with a
bottle of stolen vodka, you
whispered to the keyhole
you fucked another woman
in the alley of a rundown
bar.*

*you didn't move fast
enough, you said*

*i couldn't wait forever, you
said*

*i filled myself like a silo that
night wishing for a single
strike of lightning.*

ME: I'd prefer not to talk
about it.

ME: I'd prefer not to talk
about it.

*won't you ever get tired of
me & let me go?*

ME: it was a long time ago.

ME: it was a long time ago.

2006-2010: H

you could hear pine needles drop as you wave that pathetic dick in my face.

you clasp my hands, again, as i whisper:

what have you done to my body?

what have i done to my body?

DAD: nobody tells me
anything.

DAD: nobody tells me
anything.

In the 3rd century BC, Greek general Ptolemy I Soter ordered the construction of the Library of Alexandria, one of the first of its kind in scale and scope, to begin the process of documenting and cataloging events, cultural beliefs, political movements, weather patterns—everything. Memory finally had a place to live outside the body with a renewed hope of being carried on to future generations eager for knowledge. However, less than fifty years passed before the library was lost in a fire at the hands of Caesar.

What secrets did those ashes obliterate? What traditional rituals, mapped out on papyrus sheets, were lost to the flames lit by war?

A space was deemed necessary to collect and protect cultural objects of significance. Communities were becoming civilizations, populations shot up, and artifacts were easily lost. Museums were born to hold onto history. Now, every major city has dedicated spaces, some with a dozen or more buildings, to preserve as we continue to create.

Spaces were established, rooms dedicated to the rumination of memory. Places for people to gather and sit in a particular space and time.

A space of recall and witness.

Are you feeling entitled to my memories yet?

There is a phenomenon that occurs when you tell a memory to someone for the first time. As the neurons fire through your brain, language sputters out of you in droves as the recollection of the memory feeds quotes and settings and faces into your cortex. The smell of fresh cut peonies; the distant murmur of a commuter ferry; the exact grip and warmth of your lover's fingers braided with yours. You live in the sensations all over again it seems.

Hands flying, moments mimicked, eyes widen, a laugh rolling over words, or perhaps something gets caught on the way up… your eyes drift to the left, a process of summoning, letting the thrill of memory possess your body.

The novelty of a new memory can be seen in widening pupils, excited by the prospect of sharing a moment in your life that proves to someone you are living.

"These are the things that have happened to me since I last saw you…"

"Are we all caught up?"

You perform the memory to the best of your ability, improvising lines and expressions. One misstep will ruin the delivery, so the recollection has to be flawless.

What's the role of the person hearing a memory for the second time? Are you the one responsible for telling them you've heard this story before? You interrupt them mid-sentence, watch their face fall as you witness them think about if and when they've told you this story before. Or do you perform memory with them? Act surprised by the minute details, laugh when they laugh, rise when they rise, fill in gaps they may have forgotten.

*

FALSIFY.

I finally hit CALL and the phone rings.

"I'm so sorry to hear about grandpa."

"Yes, well…"

My grandma's voice is high and merciful, balancing between decades' practice of poise and whimsy. Her short sentences prevent me from hearing the hurt she's working hard to bury. The undercurrent of her sentences, like a riptide, threatens to pull down the polished, melodic cadence of her voice.

"I loved him so much, too. Please let me know if I can do anything for you."

"Thank you for calling."

I'm watching videos of my grandma from months ago— she's playing the piano. Dementia has yet to touch her procedural memory of ivory. A laugh escapes as she misses a key. She plays Clair de Lune like the notes live in the groves of her fingerprints. I know soon her laugh will only exist in five second soundbites right next to the voicemails I saved from grandpa.

There is a room inside her melodic laugh—

A space where she remembers what happened yesterday.

A space where she can easily recall the names of her grandchildren.

A space where her love still exists, sitting on her embroidered couch, asking for another cup of coffee. He smiles at her and she no longer remembers the feeling of waking up to cold sheets alone.

I play these videos for an hour or more

feeling like a human learning how to mourn.

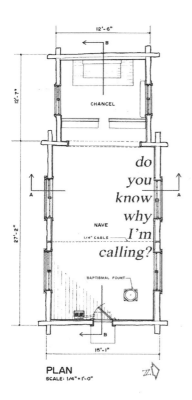

12'-6"

B

CHANCEL

*do
you
know
why
I'm
calling?*

NAVE

1/4" CABLE

A   A

12'-7"

27'-2"

BAPTISMAL FOUNT

B

15'-1"

PLAN
SCALE: 1/4" = 1'-0"

N

CROSS SECTION A-A
SCALE: 1/4" = 1'-0"

because grandma has died

EAST ELEVATION
SCALE: 1/4" = 1'-0"

Think of   living

in this small space   by mistake or on

purpose

deep

invisible tracks they must leave   behind   —

Acknowledgements

This will be long-winded. It's my first book.

This body of work took a lot out of me, both in writing and performance, and I could not have done it without many core people in my life: Chelsey, Kristine, and Sam, thank you for always reading my work and coming to my readings. Caitlin, thank you for never turning down the opportunity to make art with me, no matter what remote location it takes us to. My heart is full with all of you.

To the mentors and peers I've encountered throughout the years, each guiding me and helping me unlock my voice as a writer in a myriad of ways: Ever Jones, Corinne Manning, Sarah Dowling, Amaranth Borsuk, Rebecca Brown, Lydia K. Valentine, Suzanne Morrison, Anna Vodicka, Renee Gladman and more. To the University of Washington Tacoma Dream Team, Kari Treese and Chelsea Vitone, who read many drafts of this book, I'll love you forever. May we all continue to sip from the moon and cultivate experiences that dance on our tongues.

Thank you to my University of Washington Bothell MFA cohort for helping me through the early stages of this book, specifically Ally Morton, Yoha Cabello, and Liezel Moraleja Hackett, my cool rider. I owe you all a shot of tequila. Another one.

Thank you to the places some of this work has appeared before, some in different forms or drafts: *2018 Best American Experimental Writing Anthology*, *The Offing*, *FIVE:2:ONE Magazine*, *Heavy Feather Review*, *Glass: A Journal of Poetry*, *The Shallow Ends*, Civil Coping Mechanisms' *Shadow Map* anthology, and *Ghost Proposal*.

Many organizations have supported my work over the years and I'm immensely grateful to Artist Trust, Alma Mater, Creative Colloquy (Jackie Casella), and the community at Hugo House (Rob Arnold, Margot Kahn, Allison Augustyn, and many past and present staff and instructors).

Thank you to Jason Teal, Bill Lessard, and everyone at *Heavy Feather Review* for taking a chance on this book, for diving into every page with immense care, and for giving me agency throughout the entire publishing process. I'm glad we went on this journey together. Thank you to Katie Prince for designing the cover I envisioned in my head but never knew how to properly explain. It's perfect.

To the King County Library System: I think I owe you all money, but these research books were too good to turn back in on time. Thank you for allowing me to check out 20 books at a time and not bat an eye.

To Vintage, the coffee shop where I probably wrote most of the book. You ladies put up with a lot from me.

To Grandma and Grandpa McCarthy: you two were so hip, and we miss you everyday. I used to sit around listening to my grandpa's war stories without a care in the world, just listening to the soft cadence of his voice; the small pauses for recollection. It wasn't until he passed that I wished we had recorded every one of his stories. Sending my love to all my family in California.

Releasing a book is chaos when you're doing it alone, so I'm forever grateful to the six individuals who believed in this work and wrote beautiful blurbs to introduce it to the world:

Rebecca Brown: I always look at a sentence more than once to see if I can say what I need to say in fewer words, thanks to you. You took me and many of us into your community, and we love you. Obviously.

Amaranth Borsuk: I'm so honored to have worked with you in grad school; you truly are a visionary. You not only showed me what was possible with my writing, but you joyfully encouraged me to keep pushing boundaries.

Steven Dunn: Your books and your writing are immense inspirations to me, in addition to you being one of those honest, genuine writers that people strive to be. I'm a lifetime reader of your work.

Jenny Boully: I discovered your books throughout college and every text showed me that there was a place for me and my style of work in the world. I can't tell you how honored I am that you helped this book out, and that I finally get to shelve my book next to yours on my bookshelf.

Piper J. Daniels: GIRL. Where would this book be without you? You saw every layer of this book and what it was attempting to do, and you sang its praises even when I forgot the tune. I'm a better writer because of you. Thank you for your friendship.

Renee Gladman: I'll say it plainly—this book would not exist without you. You pushed me when you knew I had more to give, you asked for more, and you saw how much I needed to write this book. I'll be forever grateful that our paths crossed then and continue to cross now.

Thank you to my family, although I hope you guys never read this book. And thank you to my bub, Rajah.

Thank you to everyone who reads this book and encounters it with tenderness and understanding.

And to my love, Terrell: my favorite editor, biggest cheerleader, best friend, and everything in between. This book, and all the other books I have in the pipeline, could not have been written without your close eye and open heart. We are binary stars.

Notes

Carter, Rita. *Mapping the Mind*. Berkeley: University of California Press, 2010. Book.

Gordon, Barry. *Memory: Remembering and Forgetting in Everyday Life*. New York: MasterMedia Limited, 1995. Book.

Harris, William. *THE GREEK DACTYLIC HEXAMETER*. n.d. Online. September 2016.

Jacope, Annese, et al. "Nature Communications." 28 January 2014. *Nature.com*. Online. February 2017.

N.A. *https://commons.wikimedia.org/wiki/Category:Floor_plans*. n.d. Online. April 2017. [blueprints images]

Notopoulos, James A. "Mnemosyne in Oral Literature." *Transactions and Proceedings of the American Philological Association* (1938): 465-493. Online.

Plato. *Complete Works*. Indianapolis: Hackett Publishing, 1997. Book.

Squire, Larry R. "The Legacy of Patient H.M. for Neuroscience." *Cell Press* (2008): 6-9. Online Article.

Surprenant, Celine. *Freud*. London: Continuum, 2008. Book.

Tulving, Endel and Fergus I.M. Craik. *The Oxford Handbook of Memory*. New York: Oxford University Press, 2000. Book.

Whitehead, Anne. *Memory*. Abingdon: Routledge, 2009. Book. Quote from John Locke.

Photo credit: Terrell Fox

Nicole McCarthy is an experimental writer and artist based outside of Seattle. Her work has appeared in *PANK*, *Hobart*, *The Offing*, *Redivider*, *Glass: A Journal of Poetry*, *Best American Experimental Writing 2018*, and others. Her work has also been performed and encountered as projection installation pieces throughout the Puget Sound and her written work can be found at nicolemccarthypoet.com. *A Summoning* is her first book.

Made in the USA
Middletown, DE
22 July 2022

69804675R00068